The Italian Home Buyer's Guide

The definitive guide for expats and non-Italian residents to owning property in Italy

By Nicolo Bolla and Ryan Lynn

Index

Why buy a house in Italy? 3

Overview of the Italian market 4

Who can buy property in Italy? 5

Catasto? What is that? 6

Notary, what a waste of money! 8

Residency requirements. 10

Moving your residency, the right move? 12

Geometra – a unique Italian profession. 15

Non-resident bank account. 17

Capital Gain on property sale. 19

Taxation at purchase 20

Taxes at possession 23

Finance your property with a loan 27

Taxation and compliance on rent. 28

Holiday lettings – Airbnb 32

Tax deductible items at renovation 34

Buy house at auction 37

Private individual or corporation? 39

How to buy a property? 41

NPL, a different way of purchasing a property 42

Agriturismo, casa vacanze, affittacamere, B&B. 44

Esterovestizione..........50

Rent to buy guide 52

APPENDIX..........55

The Authors

Nicolo Bolla

Nicolo is from Parma, Italy. He holds a degree in Accounting, an MBA, and a Master of Accounting, along with multiple certifications. He is passionate about helping world travelers live the life they desire. Nicolo has experience helping individuals and businesses navigate tax compliance across international borders, and he is experienced in helping individuals navigate many of the financial compliance nuances of living in Italy. Among the clients Nicolo has provided services to, many have expressed a discomfort regarding the risk associated with buying property in Italy. Nicolo has helped multiple clients navigate the steps of buying an Italian home. There are many approaches to purchasing Italian property, and Nicolo has advised clients on these different approaches given their unique situation. After many successful home buying engagements for clients who were not Italian citizens, Nicolo realized the need for a definitive guide so that his advice could reach more people wishing to live their dream of becoming an Italian property owner.

Ryan Lynn

Ryan is from Pensacola, Florida. He holds an Accounting degree and MBA. Ryan is also passionate about helping world travelers live the live they desire. He is an Accounting Manager at a firm that works with businesses and individuals navigating the laws and regulations that come with being spread across multiple borders. Ryan personally provides financial advice to clients on investment strategy and believes that property ownership can be one of the most rewarding investment opportunities. Ryan is an experienced traveler himself and has traveled around the Italian peninsula multiple times. As an aspiring Italian homeowner himself, Ryan has studied the nuances of Italian property ownership for non-Italian citizens, so he will one day have the knowledge necessary to navigate the various steps required to own Italian property.

Together, Nicolo and Ryan have turned their skills, knowledge, and passion into The Italian Homebuyer's Guide to help English speakers around the world learn what steps to take toward realizing their dream of owning Italian property. We hope you enjoy this guide as much as we enjoyed creating it. The Italian Homebuyer's Guide is intended to be used as a reference for your situation, or to be read to understand the breadth of compliance regulations in the Italian real estate market.

Contact Us

Nicolo Bolla - n.bolla@accountingbolla.com

Ryan Lynn - r.lynn@accountingbolla.com

Why buy a house in Italy?

Europe's Sunny Peninsula is one of the best places in the world to become a homeowner. If you are looking for a permanent home, vacation home, or investment property, finding it in Italy will be a dream come true. Whether you like the seaside, high mountains, the immaculate countryside, crowded cities, or romantic islands, Italy has the perfect home for everyone, while also boasting a real estate market that is relatively cheap compared to most other destination countries around the world.

Furthermore, Italy is an ideal home for English speakers, as the entire countries thrives on tourism and welcoming people from around the world. Most Italians you interact with will speak proficient English and will greet you with a friendly smile, as they are eager to give you tips on how to best enjoy their home country. The public amenities and benefits are also apparent in Italy, as the country boasts efficient public transportation, clean cities and public utilities, and a healthcare system ranked among the best in the world, along with many other benefits.

The Italian lifestyle is punctuated by cultural traditions like aperitivo (Italian happy hour), long lunches, and morning espresso; traditions that are sure to make you slow down and appreciate the charm of life in Italy. In a country that has preserved its culture and history, possibly better than any other place in the world, being an Italian homeowner comes with a culturally-rich and relaxed pace of life.

The reasons for buying a home in Italy are obvious. What is not so obvious are the complicated Italian forms one must fill out and the various entities one must transact with to become an Italian homeowner. These challenges can be difficult to maneuverer, especially if you are not an Italian citizen. However, all the inevitable frustrations of the Italian housing market should not stop you from owning your dream home or becoming an Italian property investor.

There is always a solution, and if buying a home in Italy is your goal, you may be slowed down by some bureaucratic processes, but we encourage you not to let that stop you from achieving your goal. Follow along in this guide to understand the proper steps toward owning your Italian home!

How to use this guide

This guide can be read from start to finish, like a book, if you seek to educate yourself on the nuances and intricacies of the Italian property market. However, if you have specific questions regarding your situation or a client's situation, we recommend that you refer to the Table of Contents at the beginning to hone in on the exact issue you may be dealing with. If you require further assistance in solving your Italian property buying issues, please feel free to contact us by phone or email, and we invite you to visit our website to discover our premium content regarding the Italian property market.

Overview of the Italian market

After the global financial crisis of 2008, real estate prices and GDP hit rock bottom. Since then, the Italian economy has begun a path of successful recovery, and the Italian housing market has strengthened along with that recovery.

Overall, Italy has a wide and diversified real estate market the cannot be defined in only one way.

The northern regions have seen a steady increase in house prices since 2014, as well as the cities of Florence and Rome. Meanwhile, other areas of Italy are still stagnating, and prices are significantly lower than in 2008. Some other clusters have never seen a downturn in their economy, as prices and transactions always scored positive results, despite the outlook of the national market and the results in other areas of Italy.

The real estate market, just like other markets in Italy, has a strong regional connection, which is why a local real estate agent is the best resource when looking for the right property for you.

Real estate transactions have increased in the last five years, despite being far away from the levels hit during 2008, where the overall number of property transaction almost reached one million units. In 2017, 850.000 transactions were recorded in public registrars.

At this moment, Italy can provide great opportunities for investors or for people wishing to move, as prices are not fully recovered. In all the areas of the country, most market analysts have predicted a steady growth of prices in the coming years.

Furthermore, Brexit is still undergoing, and Italy can be a top destination for all the UK citizen wishing to stay in the EU.

Finally, Italy is known for its high nominal tax rate, yet Italy provides interesting tax breaks on renovation and maintenance of property, making real estate investments more attractive. In order to exploit these benefit, all you have to do is to find a reliable English-speaking accountant.

Who can buy property in Italy?

As a non-Italian resident, there might be limitations for you to purchase property located in Italy based on your citizenship or your VISA status.

There are then three possible scenarios:

1. EU citizen or EEA citizen have no limitations to purchase properties located in Italy.
2. Foreign citizen (non EU nor EEA) not holding a *Permesso di Soggiorno*, in such case the citizen can purchase a property only if an International treaty allows it or a reciprocity agreement is in place.
3. Foreign citizen (non EU nor EEA) holding a *Permesso di Soggiorno* for employment, entrepreneurship, self-employment, family, humanitarian, or study cause, living in Italy for less than three years. In such case no reciprocity nor international treaty is required.

The above conditions apply solely to individuals. Often a good way to circumvent such limitations is to establish a local corporation or a local branch of a foreign company, which can then be used as a vehicle to purchase the property.

Catasto? What is that?

The catasto is the Italian system of land registration; many other jurisdictions have a system like the Italian catasto.

The catasto is divided into two different sections:

- Catasto dei terreni (Land cadastre)
- Catasto dei fabbricati (Real estate cadastre)

Every piece of land or house in Italy has to be included in the local catasto, which is administered by the Agenzia del Territorio.

Each municipality is represented as a *Fogli mappa*, and depending on the size of the municipality, there can be more than one *Foglio mappa*.

Then, each land plot or house is defined by the following variables:

- Particella
- Subalterno
- Zona
- Micro Zona

To classify property types, Italy used a numerical classification system that is dependent on the property features. Every feature is represented by a number and the entire string of numbers is used to define a certain plot of land or house.

Furthermore, the *catasto* will provide information about every type of building with the category code made of a letter and one or two numbers. The group includes residential homes and offices.

A/01	Abitazioni di tipo signorile
A/02	Abitazioni di tipo civile
A/03	Abitazioni di tipo economico

A/04	Abitazioni di tipo popolare
A/05	Abitazioni di tipo ultrapopolare
A/06	Abitazioni di tipo rurale
A/07	Abitazioni in villini
A/08	Abitazioni in ville
A/09	Castelli, palazzi di eminenti pregi artistici o storici
A/10	Uffici e studi privati
A/11	Abitazioni ed alloggi tipici dei luoghi

Based on the category of the building and the area (or the number of rooms), the catasto will assign a cadastral value called *Rendita Catastale*.

The *Rendita Catastale* is the cornerstone value used to calculate the cadastral value which is the basis to calculate every real estate related tax as well as the Donation/Inheritance Tax.

The *catasto* is a public registrar accessible online, and you have the right to enquire it for any property. If you are in the process of evaluating a property, I advise that you put the owner's Codice Fiscale (or the house cadastral coordinates) in the system and check the information.

The *catasto* also includes information about the inside characteristics of the property, making it a fundamental resource to check the conformity of the property to the actual building.

If any discrepancy arises, the property cannot be sold, nor the deed signed.

Finally, the catasto also shows any right of any third party such as mortgages, usufruct and other rights.

Notary, what a waste of money!

This is the most common exclamation once a prospect buyer understands that the whole property deed will be performed in front of a public notary representing the Italian Republic.

I totally understand that in your home country, the process of purchasing property does not involve such a professional, but here in Italy property sales do not happen without the involvement of a notary. Take it or leave it.

At first glance, I can agree that the work performed by the notary looks wasteful and we could all be better off if we would get rid of this redundant, yet necessary, procedure.

Why is a notary important to the process?

First, the notary is impartial and represents the Italian Republic as a public official; he/she does not have any vested interest in the transactions, making sure that both parties agree to enter into the contract and understand the conditions stated in the deed.

Furthermore, the Notary ensures that the correct amount of money is paid from one party to the other, taking into account also the taxes due at purchase.

You are not required to be physically present at the signing of the deed. You can appoint a fiduciary using a procedure called *Power of Attorney*, in which you can nominate a third person to represent you in front of the Notary, giving him/her the power of signing the deed on your behalf.

What you see the day you of the deed signing is just a small part of what the Notary is required to perform in order to complete the transaction.

The Notary has to make sure that the seller has the right to sell the property and no other party nor public authority has any claim on such property, or that their written consent has been given. The Notary must make sure that the property is not frozen nor any pending judgment exists.

The Notary must also make sure that the property is in conformity with the Catasto, in case there is not a full conformity, he/she is personally liable for a wrongful transaction which should not have occurred.

There are other controls the Notary needs to perform; he/she must make sure that both parties are sound of mind, that have the authority to sign any act, and that they are not disqualified from public records.

Finally, the Notary must verify the correct tax treatment of the transaction and that the main residency benefit can be adopted for such transaction.

In the end, the Notary verifies that the full transaction abides by every applicable law acting as a law enforcement stronghold and reducing any potential future claim regarding a wrongful or fraudulent transaction. All in all, the Notary is an unbiased individual who is involved to protect both parties involved in the transaction.

Residency requirements

The requirements to become a resident of Italy vary depending on the citizenship of the applicant, in fact, the process and the requirements vary if the applicant is an Italian citizen, an EU citizen, or a non-EU citizen.

Every individual applying for residency needs to prove that he lives in property, which he has the right to live in it (ownership, rent contract, usufruct etc.) and that the property is suitable for residential use. You cannot apply for residency in a garage nor in an office!

On top of that, you are required to have a valid ID to prove your identity.

If you are an Italian citizen, valid Italian ID is all you must prove.

Non-citizens needs to prove their financial means, showing their ability to self-sustain in Italy. The requirements vary depending on the status of the applicant

EMPLOYEES

As an employee, you must show your employment contract stating that you are required to work in Italy or the object of your work in Italy.

SELF-EMPLOYED

As a self-employed worker, you are required to prove your status and provide one of the following pieces of information:

- Italian Chamber of Commerce registration
- VAT certificate
- Charter body registration

You are not required to provide every bit information, you just need one of the above, as some types of professions are not chartered or do not require a registration at the Italian Chamber of Commerce.

PENSIONER

As a pensioner wishing to move your residency to Italy, you are required to prove the source of your pension.

If you have an occupation, you are self-employed in Italy, or you have a live off a pension, it is rather easy to obtain residency in Italy.

It gets more complicated if you do not have any employment or pension and wish to live in Italy.

In such case, you are required to prove your that you can self-sustain, following the requirements in the chart below.

MINIMUM FUNDS REQUIRED	FAMILY MEMBER
€ 8.883,50	Applicant plus one family member
€ 11.778,00	Applicant plus two or more sons under the age of 14
€ 14.722,50	Applicant plus two or more sons under the age of 14 and a family member older than 14

The funds must be deposited into an Italian bank account and disclosed to process the request.

A further complication is the health coverage. Before applying for your residency, you also must subscribe to health insurance to cover you up to the day you will become a resident in Italy.

Proving health coverage is also a requirement that applies to pensioners.

The same rules apply to non-EU citizens. Non-EU citizens must go through an immigration process to obtain a VISA that allows them to move to and live in Italy. When applying for Italian residency, you are required to show the *Permesso di Soggiorno* demonstrating your right to live in Italy.

Is moving your residency the right move?

Purchasing a house and then moving your residency is a brilliant tax strategy, in fact, you will usually see a significant tax reduction as shown in the figures below:

TAX	AMOUNT
REGISTRAR TAX	2%
CADASTRAL TAX	€ 50
MORTGAGE TAX	€ 50

If the property requires VAT to be paid, taxes are as follows:

TAX	AMOUNT
REGISTRAR TAX	€ 200
CADASTRAL TAX	€ 200
MORTGAGE TAX	€ 200
VAT	4%

Furthermore, you are not required to move your residency to the purchased property, as you can do it also use a different property in the same municipality, you then have 18 months from the purchase date to file a request of residency.

The registrar tax is calculated on the cadastral value (valore catastale) of the property calculated as follows:

$Rendita\ Catastale \times 1.05 \times 110$

VAT is calculated on the price paid by the buyer, regardless of the valore catastale.

If you already have a main residency (Prima Casa), and you decide to buy a new house, you can still benefit from the reduced tax rate, as long as you sell the old property within one year of the purchase of the new property; otherwise you will be required to pay the tax savings that are wrongfully deducted, on top of a 30% sanction and legal interests.

On top of that, no property tax is paid on the main residency property.

Many people rush their decision of moving their residency to Italy solely on the ground of a tax saving on the property purchase. I encourage you to see the bigger picture once you move your residency to Italy.

According to the art. 2 TUIR (Italian tax code) an individual is considered to be resident if:

"for the greater part of the tax period, he or she is registered with the register of the resident population (anagrafe) or has their domicile or residence, as defined in the Civil Code, in the territory of the Italian state".

This means that a person is tax resident if, for the greater part of any tax year, the individual:

1. is registered in register of the resident population maintained by the local municipality "*comune*"; or
2. has his or her "*domicilio*" - their centre of vital interests; or
3. has their habitual place of abode; in Italy.

Thus, tax residence is a matter of fact. It is not a question of choice.

The main consequence is that the individual now becomes a tax resident of Italy and he/she has to declare the worldwide income thus paying taxes on all the income anywhere made in the world.

This decision will greatly affect your tax position as the Italian tax office has enough ground to claim whichever income you make all over the world, regardless of the actual number of days you decide to live in Italy.

During my career, I have seen various cases in which a foreign individual was registered at the local anagrafe in Italy, meanwhile residing full time abroad. After some years, the Italian tax office sent them a letter stating that they did not file their taxes or that they did file their taxes but did not include their foreign sourced income.

All of them claimed they had not spent more than 183 days in Italy and so they should not be considered residents for tax purposes. Unfortunately, they forgot the first condition of the article 2, being registered for more than 183 days at local municipality.

Your only relief is the Double Tax Treaty between Italy and your other residency country, yet I have to say that there could be a beneficial option to properly filing taxes in both countries, assuming that you are not double taxed on the same income.

I suggest that you audit yourself and consider the financial impact of moving to Italy. If you plan this move in advance you can move to Italy safely without any unwanted surprises or tax liabilities.

Geometra – a unique Italian profession.

The process of buying a house differs from country to country, along with the certified professionals involved. In most countries, you contact a real estate agent and a legal practitioner or lawyer to find the right home and to disentangle any potential legal complications linked to the purchase, such as liabilities still attached to the property from the former owner.

The Italian real estate industry requires a unique professional: the *Geometra*. The Geometra's involvement in the buying process is of paramount importance to any potential buyer. The Geometra is certified in both topography and legal skills specifically related to property transactions. Most importantly for any potential buyer, since the Geometra is a certified expert and is frequently involved in local property transactions, he/she is a valuable resource to estimate the value of any property, making the Geometra a critical person in helping you get the best possible deal.

Buyers often hire a Geometra after the buying process is over, yet my most valuable advice to clients is to hire a Geometra before buying your house! Involving the Geometra before inquiring about housing prices ensures that the negotiating price range will not become inflated.

The Geometra can assess if there is any other individuals or corporations that have claim to the property, or part of it. Furthermore, he/she has access to the *Catasto* to verify that the property map corresponds to the property and if any map-amendment has to be made, ensuring that you do not run into the mishap of find out that the property lines are different than what you expected after the property has been purchased.

The Geometra can assess the required maintenance to be performed, helping you determine the gravity and the impact of the potential repairs. Sometimes, especially in historical neighbourhoods, there are many limitations on the renovations and restoration to be undertaken on such buildings, which the Geometra will be pricy to.

You don't want to pay for a property that falls apart after you sign the deed, and you want to know what renovations you can and cannot make to the property.

Finally, the Geometra can perform some projects and planning on your building, if it does not involve any structural work, to help you renovate you home to your desires.

As you might have understood, the Geometra is not a lawyer, an engineer, an architect, or real estate agent, yet the Geometra can help you avoid the pitfalls and headaches that many first time Italian homebuyers experience.

Non-resident bank account.

If you have made the decision to buy a house in Italy, you are very likely to pay a down payment upfront while signing the deed. The amount of the required down payment varies depending on the area in which you decide to buy property, as well as the type of the property you buy.

This payment is very easy to execute as you can set up a bank wire from your foreign bank account to the seller's bank account. At this point, the last step is to sign the deed in front of the notary, which I again remind you can be executed by a another person whom you give *power of attorney*.

Sometimes, real estate agents fail to disclose that you are required to pay the balancing payment and the taxes due, and that the only way to make that payment is by using an old-school payment document that is required by Italian Law, the assegno circolare.

The assegno circolare is not a bank check, the issuing bank guarantees the funds to be available, thus reducing the chances of a bounce back to 0%.

But why would the notary only accept this old-fashioned payment method? It is a means of reducing risk. The assegno circolare verifies that the money is guaranteed by the bank, so the Notary can be 100% sure he/she is not a victim of a fraudulent scheme.

Now comes the tricky part! The notary only accepts the assegno circolare. To obtain an assegno circolare, you need to have a local bank account. If you walk into the local bank, especially in smaller cities, the local clerk cannot process your request if you are not a resident of Italy, and they only work with local bank accounts.

If you try to ask your foreign bank, it will not help you through the process. Even if you can get such a check from a non-Italian bank, the Italian notary will likely turn it down as the bank is not Italian.

It sounds like you might reach a dead end at this point, and you cannot get the house you already put a down payment on, nor can you get the down payment back.

This can be a nightmare scenario for a non-Italian resident, and one that may spoil your dream of becoming an Italian homeowner! Thankfully there is a solution.

The solution is a non-resident bank account.

The non-resident bank account is, as the word says, a bank account for individuals who do not have a residency in Italy, and it is run by a local authorized bank, thus solving any potential denials of you right to the property.

All you need to setup a non-resident bank account is:

- Codice Fiscale (which you also need to buy a property)
- Valid ID
- Proof of residency abroad

With this information and a bunch of signatures, you will then have an Italian based bank account that works the same as a resident bank account.

Now all you must do is transfer funds from your foreign bank account to the Italian one, and when you are ready to sign the deed, you need to ask you bank for the assegno circolare.

Despite the fact that the non-resident bank account is more expensive than the local ones (from € 5.00 to € 20.00 in monthly fees), this is the fastest and safest way to handle a property purchase in Italy if you are a non-resident; finally, once you become a resident in Italy, you can turn your bank account into a local one, saving on the monthly fees.

If you decide not to become a resident of Italy you can keep the non-resident account, so you can domicile you bills, utilities, and your property tax payments while you are abroad.

Capital Gain on property sale

If you decide to sell your property, you may be liable to pay income tax on your capital gain. If the property is owned by a corporation, the capital gain is always taxable, whereas as an individual your capital gain might be tax exempt.

The rule of thumb is that if you sell your property five years after the purchase deed date, your capital gain is not taxable, regardless of the amount and the type of property. If you sell your property within five years' time, you are liable to pay income tax on your capital gain.

As a taxpayer, you can opt for two types of taxation on your capital gain. The first one is the regular IRPEF (Italian income tax) progressive brackets starting from 23% up to 43% on top of any regional and municipal surcharge applicable; this capital gain will cumulate with any other income made, moving the taxpayer towards the higher tax brackets

The second option is a flat 20% substitute tax on your capital gain.

Unlike other jurisdictions the whole capital gain is taxed in full in a single tax year; it is not possible to carry-back nor carry-forward such type of income.

It seems obvious to opt for the 20% substitute tax as the tax basis is the same and IRPEF has higher brackets, though you should not rush your decision.

The IRPEF tax allows for deductible items and tax credit reductions, whereas the substitute tax does not allow it. It is therefore crucial to liaise with your tax accountant to understand what your net tax cost is.

Let's look at a hypothetical scenario to better understand the nuances of this topic. If you buy a residential property as your main residence and decide to sell it within five years of the purchase deed, you might be exempt from a capital gain tax if you meet both the following conditions:

1. Your residency was in that house for the majority of your ownership period.
2. You purchase a new property as main residency within one year of the sale deed.

Taxation at purchase

If you purchase property in Italy, you are required to pay different taxes that very depending on the type of property and the classification of the seller.

RESIDENTIAL PROPERTY

If you purchase residential property from a private individual or from a company that does not charge Value Added Tax (VAT), the following taxes are payable.

TYPE OF TAX	AMOUNT
IMPOSTA DI REGISTRO	9% of the cadastral value
IMPOSTA IPOTECARIA	€ 50,00
IMPOSTA CATASTALE	€ 50,00

If the seller is a company charging VAT, the following taxes are payable.

TYPE OF TAX	AMOUNT
IVA	10% of the property value (22% if the property belongs to A/01-A/08-A/09)
IMPOSTA DI REGISTRO	€ 200,00
IMPOSTA IPOTECARIA	€ 200,00
IMPOSTA CATASTALE	€ 200,00

It is possible to reduce taxes payable at purchase if the residential property is elected as *main residency*. In such a case, taxes are as follows:

TYPE OF TAX	AMOUNT
IMPOSTA DI REGISTRO	2% of the cadastral value
IMPOSTA IPOTECARIA	€ 50,00

| IMPOSTA CATASTALE | € 50,00 |

If the seller is a company charging VAT, the following taxes are payable.

TYPE OF TAX	AMOUNT
IVA	4% of the property value
IMPOSTA DI REGISTRO	€ 200,00
IMPOSTA IPOTECARIA	€ 200,00
IMPOSTA CATASTALE	€ 200,00

To benefit from the main residency tax reduction, the buyer is required to move his/her residency to the same municipality in which the property is located within 18 months of the date on the purchase deed.

As a buyer, you are not required to move to the property you purchased, for the simple fact that your property might require renovations that take longer than 18 months.

Failure to move your residency within 18 months of the purchase deed will make you liable to pay the difference between the taxes paid and the taxes payable on top of a fine amounting to 30% of any tax due.

VAT can only be charged if the seller is a trading entity. The seller has the obligation to charge VAT if the property has been completed within 5 years from the deed date, in any other case, the seller can opt to waive VAT.

COMMERCIAL AND INDUSTRIAL PROPERTY

If you are interested in purchasing any commercial or industrial property, I advise you to do so through a trading entity (partnership or corporation) as the taxes payable at purchase are relevant.

Commercial or residential property sold by the builder to a trading entity

TYPE OF TAX	AMOUNT
IVA	10% or 22% of the property value
IMPOSTA DI REGISTRO	€ 200,00
IMPOSTA IPOTECARIA	3%
IMPOSTA CATASTALE	1%

If the buyer is an individual, then the VAT is waived only if the sale occurs more than 5 years after the completion of the property.

The same rules apply to other trading entities, which are required to charge VAT within 5 years after the property completion, in every other case the buyer can opt to waive the VAT.

When purchasing such a type of property as a trading entity you do not technically "pay" VAT as the whole transaction is made through the *reverse charge* option.

Taxes at possession

Once you buy property, you are liable to pay taxes based on the possession. These taxes are set out by the national government, and they are administered by the local municipality in which the property is located. Taxes are:

- Imposta Municipale Unica (IMU)
- Tassa sui Servizi Indivisibili (TASI)
- Tassa sui Rifiuti (TARI)

Years ago, Italy had a fully centralized tax system and the tax collection was a sole responsibility of the central government, then taxing authorities were transferred to the local, regional, and municipal authorities.

During recent years, there has been a push towards a more decentralized tax system, thus increasing the budget spending and the responsibility of the local administrators who are required to levy and collect local taxes.

Property tax is among the most important local taxes, and each *comune* has the power to increase or reduce the tax bracket, as well as provide reductions and deductions based on different characteristics of the property or the use of the property itself.

Imposta Municipale Unica (IMU)

The IMU is by far the most important property tax, and it is levied on the ownership of a property (land, residential property, commercial and industrial property) located in Italy.

IMU is paid in two instalments, the first one is payable on/before June 16th – January to June ownership – while the second one is payable on/before December 16th – July to December ownership.

The government determines the formula to calculate the value on which to apply the IMU bracket

$IMU\ value = Rendita\ Catastale \times 1,05 \times Coefficient$

The coefficient is determined on the type of the property

160	Group A buildings (excluding A/10) and C/02, C/06, C/07
140	Group B buildings and C/03, C/04, C/05
80	A/10 and D/05 buildings
65	Group D buildings (excluding D/05)
55	C/01
135	Agricultural land

Tax brackets are determined at the national level; however, every council can increase or reduce its value based on their resolution. In any case, it is not possible to exceed the cap of 1,06%.

The national brackets are determined as follows:

0,4%	Main residency property
0,2%	Agricultural property
0,76%	Every other property

The council resolution also determines the possible exemption or reduction of IMU payable based on certain circumstances. Since it is not possible to explain every possible reduction or exemption, I am recapping the most common ones:

- Residential property rented as main residency for the tenant
- Residential property rented to University students
- Residential property rented at a lower than market rate
- Residential property rented to a 1st degree family member
- Commercial property rented to young entrepreneurs

Furthermore, there are two reductions dictated at the national level:

1. Main residency ("prima casa") property.
2. Any property rented under the *"canone concordato"*.

In the first case no IMU is levied, in the second case the IMU bracket is reduced of 25%.

Finally, if a property is not fit for use requiring major repairs or maintenance to be habitable or exploitable, no IMU is payable.

Let's do some math!

Assume you own a residential property in Milan with a *Rendita Catastale* of € 511,29.

Your property IMU value is € 85.896,72

Formula = € 511,29 x 1,05 x 1,06

Assuming this property is your main residency, you are not required to pay any IMU.

If your property is not your main residency the tax bracket is 1,06% hence the IMU payable is calculated as € 910,50 per year.

If your property is rented under a *Canone Concordato,* the bracket is reduced to 0,80%, and the IMU payable is € 682,88

TASI

TASI was introduced in 2014 and it is not technically a property tax. TASI finances the general services provided by the local council (local police, local demography service, local road repairs and maintenance etc.); if you are familiar with the English council tax, TASI operates in the same way.

Unlike IMU, TASI is also payable by the occupant of the property.

TASI ranges from a minimum of 0,08% up to 0,33% based on the council resolution; furthermore, the sum of IMU and TASI cannot exceed the statutory limit of 1,14%.

TASI calculation base is the same as IMU, as well as the payments deadlines.

Depending on the municipality resolution the tenant of a property might be required to pay TASI on a pro quota basis ranging from 10% up to 30% of any TASI due.

TARI

TARI is the waste collection tax and it is solely payable by the occupant of the property, and if the property is not occupied by anyone, the owner is then responsible.

Unlike IMU and TASI, TARI is calculated on the number of the occupants of the house and it is calculated and sent to your residential address by the local multi-utility company that is in charge of administering the waste collection (based on the area these companies usually run the electricity, water, and other energy resources supply).

Often times, the local *comune* assumes a number of occupants based on their resolution; if fewer people are registered in that property, then you can notify the local *comune* amending the amount of TARI due.

TARI comes in two equal instalments payable during the month of May and the month of November.

Every aforementioned tax is calculated on a monthly basis. If you purchase the property during the year then you have to apportion your tax due on the months of possession.

According to the law, if you are required to pay a full month of tax if you signed the property purchase deed between the 1st day of the month up to the 15th day of the same month; if you sign it from the 16th day on, you are not required to pay the full month of tax.

Finance your property with a loan

Buyers often do not have enough resources to pay for a property at purchase hence they recur to financial institution that can help them.

As a foreign individual, it is more complicated for you to get access to bank loans and mortgages due to multiple barriers such as the low knowledge of the Italian banking system, the poor understanding of the English language by most Italian professionals, as well as the absence of any significant income in Italy. All these factors, among others, can greatly harm your possibility of securing a bank mortgage, hence you are very likely to give up to your dream house.

During the years I have heard multiple unpleasant stories from non-Italian speakers trying to secure a loan through an Italian bank. It is a fact that many local Italian banks do not want to deal with clients they do not know or they are barely known; furthermore, the Italian banks have changed their attitude towards lending after the big financial crisis of 2008.

Long story short, it is more difficult to get money from Italian banks nowadays.

All I can say about this situation is that the DIY approach often fails, all you have to do is rely on a trusted professional (tax accountant, lawyer, real estate agent, geometra etc.) that can introduce you to a local bank and explain your situation and try work and negotiate on the terms of loan.

Already being a client of that bank usually helps and can speed up the process, if you signed a non-resident bank account they already know you and you could have an advantage.

In my experience, I have helped hundreds of individuals and companies secure funding through financial institutions as long as the buyer was willing to put a down payment of 20%.

Often times, the buyer was not even resident in Italy nor had income here! Many times, a foreign payslip was sufficient proof of the credit worthiness!

Finally, if you buy your main residency, many banks have lower rates and the 0,25% loan tax is waived and the interest paid is tax deductible.

Taxation and compliance on rent

If you decide to rent a property, you are required to draft and sign a property lease. Unlike other jurisdictions, Italy requires the lease agreement to be in a written form and to abide by multiple features as determined by the law. Furthermore, the length of the lease is not a free arrangement between the parties, having some statutory limitations; you will often hear the formula 4+4, 3+2 or 6+6.

The first two formulas refer to residential property leases, meaning that the property is rented for four (or three) years with a silent renewal of extra four (or two) years; this does not mean that you are bound to the contract for its whole duration. Usually the lease contract includes the early termination clause, allowing the tenant to terminate the contract with early notice.

I will introduce you to the main duties required to lease a property and the taxes payable in the process. The contracts can be divided into two different categories: residential and non-residential.

This chapter only refers to lease agreements longer than 30 days, which are included in the holiday lettings contracts.

Regardless of the type of lease, every contract needs to be registered with the *Agenzia delle Entrate* within 30 days of the signature.

You can register the contract at the local tax office, or you can do everything online by yourself (if you have the credentials to access the Agenzia delle Entrate), or you can delegate to your tax accountant, real estate agent, or Geometra to register the contract on your behalf.

If any tax is payable, you are required to pay it at registration.

RESIDENTIAL LEASE

The residential lease provides multiple taxation options depending on the articles of the contract. First of all, the residential lease contract has fixed duration as the law states it at 4 years renewable of other 4 years or a reduced duration of 3 years renewable of extra two years. A further option exists for contracts lasting less than 12 months, this option is called *contratto transitorio* requiring to tenant to have some employment, family, or study reasons to rent a property for less than the statutory terms.

The fact that the contract might last up to 8 years does not mean that you cannot terminate it earlier, in fact you can do it based on the advance notice written in the contract; sometimes it is a short one-month notice, sometimes it is a longer period. There is no legal requirement to set a minimum or maximum advance notice period.

If the contract does not fit the aforementioned rules, the tenant can terminate it at any time and he/she is not bound to the conditions set in the agreement. Take great care when drafting or signing a lease! If you do not know what each condition entails, ask the advice of a professional.

As far as taxes, the landlord can opt between two options:

1. Regime Ordinario
2. Cedolare Secca

Both tax regimes have impact on income tax, registrar tax, and stamp duty.

Let's consider a residential lease contract worth € 6000 per year by a private individual.

REGIME ORDINARIO

The regime ordinario entails that the rental income is taxed based on the IRPEF brackets and it cumulates with other incomes (employment income, finance income, other income etc.) to calculate the gross income on which the progressive IRPEF brackets are calculated.

On top of that *imposta di registro* and *imposta di bollo* are due at registration, as well as the *imposta di registro* is due every year and at early termination.

Every year, the landlord can adjust the annual lease value based on the national inflation index.

At registration, the *imposta di registro* is calculated as 2% of the annual lease value while the *imposta di bollo* is calculate at € 12 every 4 pages of contract (or 100 lines) per copy; assuming a standard 8 pages contract and two copies the total stands at € 48.

Imposta di registro   € 120,00

Imposta di bollo   € 48,00

TOTAL   **€ 168,00**

The € 168,00 are split equally between the landlord and the tenant.

From now on, the landlord (or the tenants) needs to pay the 2% imposta di registro every year for a total of € 120,00 split equally between the two. Finally, if any of the parties wish to terminate the contract earlier than its natural termination date, a payment of € 67,00 is required and it is split between the landlord and the tenant.

As far as income taxes, the rental income is taxable for 95% of the annual value; the 5% reduction granted by law is supposed to cover the landlord's expenses. No expense can be written off against the lease value.

In our case, the taxable income is € 5970,00 and it is taxed based on the marginal IRPEF bracket, starting from 23% up to 43% on top of any regional and municipal surcharge.

The best possible scenario is that the minimum tax payable is € 1373,10 plus any regional and municipal surcharge.

CEDOLARE SECCA

This residential property tax regime was introduced in 2011, providing great simplifications to both the landlord and the tenant.

This regime is applicable only to residential properties and to individuals, meaning that if any of the parties is a society, partnership, or corporation, the *cedolare secca* cannot be applied.

No *imposta di registro* nor *imposta di bollo* is levied at registration, anniversary, or early termination; cedolare secca requires the landlord to pay taxes only on income.

Furthermore, it does not allow the landlord to adjourn the lease value based on the Italian inflation index.

The Cedolare Secca is a flat 21% substitute tax on rent, regardless of the tax bracket in which that income falls.

In our case the taxable income is € 6000,00 and the tax paid € 1260,00 with no regional nor municipal surcharge.

Why would anyone opt for the ordinary regime? The income tax is higher, and you are required to pay a tax every year on the annual lease increasing the administrative costs. No healthy mind should ever opt for the ordinary regime, but there is a catch.

The main downside of the Cedolare Secca is that it does not come with any tax deductions.

Imagine now that your only source of income is this rental income.

In such case, your taxable income € 5970,00 and your gross tax is € 1373,10, however the tax system grants you a tax deduction of € 1077,61, leaving you out to pay only € 295,49.

Moreover, if you have any tax-deductible expense (house renovation, health and vet expenses, life insurance etc.) you can further reduce your tax payable.

The conclusion is that the Cedolare Secca is always convenient to individuals who have income in higher brackets and that cannot exploit many tax-deductible items.

In any case, I strongly advise you to liaise with your tax accountant to understand the tax implications of your rental income and how to minimize your tax liability.

NON-RESIDENTIAL PROPERTY

The non-residential property lease does not provide the landlord to opt for the Cedolare Secca, leaving the ordinary regime as the only viable option.

Finally, if the landlord is a trading entity and not a private individual, it is possible that it charges VAT on the contract.

In such case, if the property is residential, the tenant can opt for VAT exemption.

If the VAT is charged in the contract, the *imposta di registro* is reduced to 1%.

Holiday lettings – Airbnb

During the 2017 fiscal year, the Italian government introduced new tax rules to regulate the growing online booking portal, which is why this law is often referred as the "Airbnb law". This law regulated the holiday lettings since there were little to no tax and legal obligations for lettings lasting less than 30 days each.

A few year ago, this market was a minimal part of the overall rental market, yet due to the growth of the sharing economy and the introduction of global key players such as Airbnb, Bookings, etc., this market has boomed, and the Italian government decided to regulate it in order not to lose any potential tax revenue.

According to the law, any residential lease or sublease contract fitting the following features:

- Duration not exceeding the 30 days
- Signed after July 1st 2017
- Residential property contract
- The contract might include ancillary services (room cleaning, Wi-Fi, landline phone etc.)
- Landlord does not act as a trading entity

Qualifies for the holiday lettings scheme.

Such scheme allows the landlord to opt for the *Cedolare Secca* regime or for the IRPEF case by case when filing the annual tax return.

It is up to you to decide which part of income tax through the cedolare secca or through the regular IRPEF brackets.

It is not possible to deduct any type of expense incurred for the lettings as it is not a business activity.

As said earlier, no tax is calculated on the ancillary services provided to the hosts.

If your bookings are managed by a third-party portal that manages the whole booking process as well as the payments and refunds, the portal itself is required to withhold 21% of taxes as a prepayment on the taxes you owe to the Italian government.

At the end of the tax year, the online portal should send you a document recapping the total amount of taxes withheld during the same tax year (the document is called *Certificazione Unica*).

Until recently, the online portal did not operate any tax withheld on their bookings, they are currently undergoing major lawsuits with the Italian government as they do not want to abide to this new ruling, which, according to them, is nonsense.

As for now, you must include your holiday lettings income in your tax return and decide what amount you wish to tax, dependent upon which tax regime applies to your situation, then pay your taxes.

Once the portals will withhold your tax, you should also include that in your tax return and deduct that amount from the tax payable to reduce your tax liability.

Tax deductible items at renovation

Every house requires renovation or restoration from time to time. The Italian government has set up a series of tax incentives to facilitate house renovations, seismic structural improvements, and energy efficient investments.

The whole rationale behind this choice is to reduce the damages and risks caused by aged properties and to reduce the potential victims due to seismic events, which from time to time hit Italy in different areas.

Before explaining the different types of tax deductions, I would like to identify who can benefit of such deductions.

REMEMBER: In order to benefit of the tax deductions, you need to pay IRPEF in Italy!

The following categories:

1. Owner
2. Usufruct holder
3. Tenant
4. Partnerships and corporations
5. Civil union partner
6. Family member of the owner

The tax-deductible expenses refer to:

- Extraordinary maintenance
- Energy efficiency investments
- Restoration and renovation
- Seismic improvements

These expenses are tax deductible if referred to a single property or to the common areas of a condominium.

The maximum amount of tax deductible expense is € 96.000,00 per property; the tax-deductible part is generally 50% and it is discounted in 10 years.

Assuming you have paid € 20.000,00 to renovate your property, the total tax deduction is € 10.000,00. Since you will benefit this tax saving for the following 10 years you will save € 1.000,00 in tax every tax year.

All you have to do is to pay the invoice using a special type of bank transfer called *"bonifico ristrutturazioni"*, file your taxes, and the keep the proper documentation for inspection.

In the previous case, you have to make sure that you pay at least € 1.000,00 per year in tax.

Assuming your gross tax liability is € 900,00, your tax liability will drop to € 0, but you have no chance to recoup the € 100,00 unused tax deduction.

If the same investments would have been done into new solar panels, the tax-deductible part is raised to 65%. Considering your initial investment of € 20,000.00, you are entitled to a tax credit of € 13.000,00 to be used in ten years, hence € 1.300,00 per year.

If you spend money on seismic improvements to your property, the tax-deductible part is raised to 70% of the expenditure if the seismic rate increases of one category. A further raise to 80% is granted if the seismic rate improves of two categories.

An extra 5% benefit is granted to condominium properties, adjusting the tax-deductible part to 75% and 85% respectively.

Contrary to the previous tax-deductible items, the seismic improvement expenses are deductible in 5 years.

Assuming an expenditure of € 80.000,00 that increases the seismic rate of one category, the tax-deductible part is € 56.000,00. In such case, you can benefit of a tax credit amounting to € 11.200,00 every year.

As you might understand, every time you decide to renovate your property you have to talk to your tax accountant to understand if you pay enough tax to have a substantial benefit from such renovations.

It is also possible to "pay" the individual or the company performing the works with the tax credit, transferring the right to deduct such expenses in their tax return, rather than in yours. I personally know few companies that use the technique, but this can also be a good option to optimize each other's taxes.

Buying a house at an auction

Italy, like many other countries, has recently faced a disproportionate crisis of the real estate market consequential to the 2008 global financial crisis. The result of the financial crisis is the surge in the auction market for houses, as more individuals and companies could not pay their mortgages, the bank decided to exert the foreclosure right and sell the property at auction.

During the recent years, many individuals and companies have populated the auction market, allowing the buyers to make find bargains.

Before deciding to buy a property at auction, great care must be taken. Unlike the free market transaction, the auction market is a highly regulated procedure overseen by a judge and the local tribunal.

As required by the law, every house in auction must be publicly available on the Internet, as well as in local journal, providing a brief description of the house and the contacts to ask for information and organise a visit to property before the auction.

Visiting the property is essential to get a taste of the potential of the property, it is free of charge and you can collect valuable relevant information. There could be glaring things that stand out when you see a house in-person that could go unnoticed when you only see it online. While a housing auction can seem hectic and force parties to act hastily, it is not uncommon for people to act too carelessly and wind up purchasing a home that is grossly overvalued, simply because they did not take the time to go see it in-person.

Every auction comes with a tribunal resolution describing every relevant element of the property, including the map, the location, the property description, the occupancy status, and any other relevant information for the prospect auctioneers. Of course, the price is set by the tribunal and usually is way below the market value. This is the most attractive aspect of the auction market, if you do your homework, you can walk away with a very favourable deal.

Before placing an offer, I suggest you to undertake the following steps:

- Ask a Geometra for a due diligence of the property, assessing the congruence of the price.
- Make sure you have enough money to cover the price and the taxes.
- Check if the house is transferred free of the current occupants.

Once you have gone through this checklist and you are satisfied with the outcome, it is time to focus on your offer.

First, read the tribunal resolution and understand how to place an offer and the ultimate deadline; any late offer will be disregarded.

The offer must be presented in a white sealed envelope containing the participation form, a valid ID and the *assegno circolare* of a 10% down payment. The sealed envelope must be delivered to the Tribunal 24 hours before the auction day.

Since January 1st 2018 it is possible to place offers online if the tribunal resolution considers this possibility.

On the auction day, the judge or the notary opens every letter, checks the formalities, and assigns the property to the highest offer.

An offer to be valid must not be inferior to 75% of the advertised price.

If no one shows up at the auction date, the price is reduced of 25%. After three deserted auctions the property is sold in auction starting from € 1.

Assuming you have now won your auction (Hurray!) you have 60 to 90 days to provide the whole sum required to pay the property.

Buying your property at auction does not provide you any tax incentive, as the main taxes are applicable to auction sales as well. The best advantage of an auction is that the property deed is free as the judge transfers the property without the intervention of a Notary.

My keenest advice to you is to go through the whole process (at least the first time!) with the help of one or more professional since it is very easy to make rookie mistakes.

The best deal is the right one. Do not forget it!

Private individual or corporation?

As a tax accountant, I always receive the following question: "Would you suggest me to setup a corporation to buy property?" The answer is always very simple. I do not know!

Do not misunderstand me, I am not a lazy professional wishing to dodge a complicated answer, yet I have not enough information to provide a suitable and meaningful answer.

All I can do is to highlight the main key points to help you decide whether it is better to buy your property as a corporation rather than do it as an individual. Depending on you unique situation, one may be more valuable than the other, so you can say that when it comes to whether it is more beneficial to buy a property as an individual or as a corporation, it depends.

As you might have understood, it is not possible for individuals to write off expenses incurred for the property itself. All repairs, maintenance, improvements and other expenses do not create any tax advantage if you act as an individual; as a corporation you can deduct them from your revenues.

Corporations can also write off multiple other expenses such as the administrative expenses and any other expenses incurred to carry out business activities, thus reducing the taxable profit.

On the other hand, capital gains are always taxable if realized by a corporation, while if realized by an individual are only taxable if sold within 5 years from the purchase deed; furthermore, the main residency tax advantages only apply to individuals.

In regards to renovation expenses, those can be tax deductible for individuals at a rate of 50% of the expense incurred, while corporations can expense it every tax year.

Corporations, on the other hand, can deduct every tax paid at purchase as well as the IMU paid, moreover corporations can also deduct the depreciation of the property acquired during every tax year. Individuals have no such option.

Corporations can also deduct VAT paid and charge for VAT while individuals have no opportunity to recover any of the VAT paid.

Accounting fees are much higher for corporations than for individuals, as corporation are required to be VAT compliant, file the annual accounts, and file the annual tax return.

A final consideration I want you take regarding the wind-up process of a corporation: if the corporation owns any tangible property, the corporation cannot be wound-up; this factor usually increases the time and the costs required to end corporation's existence.

As you can tell, there is no answer to the question above, yet I have outlined several issues you can work on to better understand if the corporation is what you need. Talk with your tax accountant and he/she will be able to point you in the right direction to minimize your tax expenditure.

NPL, a different way of purchasing a property

NPL stands for Non-Performing Loans; you might be familiar with such acronym after the global financial crisis, as global financial institutions had to deal with many of them after their clients defaulted on mortgage payments.

NPL used to be accessible only to large institutional investors, which would make a great discount offer to buy the defaulted credit and rearrange the terms of payment with the debtors, virtually turning it into a financing transaction.

After the recent EU resolution called MIFID II introducing new stringent ratios for greater stability, NPL became literally of no interest for banking institutions as they cannot be used anymore to backup loans paid out.

At this point banks are not holding NPLs anymore. Banks have also opened the market to private investors. In other words, banks will accept offers to buy NPLs from anyone.

Before explaining you how to find great deals with the NPL market, I have to warn you that this is a rather complicated transaction. A successful transaction always involves multiple professionals. Usually banks offer discounts up to 70% of the outstanding capital to private investors.

As a private investor, you must have a clear picture of your total budget, what type of property are you interested in, and what your long-term goal is with such property (flip over, resell, living in, renting, etc.).

Now that you have a clear plan, you can enquire to the bank. Banks, unlike real estate agents, do not advertise for such deals, so you must know the right people in the financing institutions.

I have overseen hundreds of NPLs transactions, and I am now able to help buyers look for their property due to the extensive work made with multiple financing institutions.

Assuming you have found the property you are interested in, and you agree with the price, it is about time to understand how to technically seal the deal.

The bank is not selling you a property, it is selling a defaulted credit backed up by a property. This makes a huge difference! I have seen many individuals strike amazing deals by executing the takeover of an NPL.

To evaluate whether or not an NPL is right for you, compare the property market value and what you paid, since bank's discount offering is on the outstanding loan, not on the property itself. Furthermore, you have to make sure the debtor is still in the property or there was an eviction.

Now you have two options:

1. Keep the loan and ask for payments
2. Redeem the property and evict the debtor

Usually people are more interested in option number 2 as they are looking for a property.

In such a case, you must make sure to reach an agreement with the debtor. Usually the agreement is that you will take the property and the debtor walks out of it without any foreclosure or legal actions.

Once you have a binding agreement with the debtor, you can purchase your NPL and in a couple of months you will be the official owner of the property, free to live, rent, make improvements, or anything else you see fit as the property's new owner.

Once again, I would like to stress the importance of professional support. It is very easy to fall into legal and technical mistakes that can turn your investment into a bad deal.

At least the first time, avoid the DIY approach.

Agriturismo, casa vacanze, affittacamere, B&B.

Many people moving to Italy are willing to lease part of their properties, or they are keen to invest in a property to lease out to tourists.

The most common options are:

- Agriturismo
- Casa Vacanze
- Affittacamere
- B&B

Each option is considered a professional occupation, unlike the Airbnb lettings which falls outside of the scope of a professional activity. This decision will have implications on your tax affairs as well as the Social Security and government retirement benefits.

AGRITURISMO

Agriturismo, or farming hospitality, is a type of touristic lettings available in connection with agricultural activities, meaning that only a professional agricultural entrepreneur can enter into such business.

The recent years trend in Italian tourism has shown an increasing awareness and success of the ecologic and country tourism, making agriturismo a more successful form of hospitality.

This type of business is regulated by regional authorities. At this moment, I can only provide an overview of it as it varies depending on regional regulations. It should be noted that establishing your agriturismo in Lombardy or Apulia might be different.

Agriturismo is a complimentary activity to the agricultural one, meaning you cannot start an official agriturismo without any farming connected activity, which also includes taking advantage of the multiple tax breaks, benefits, and subsidies available to such types of accommodation.

The core business is the hospitality one, yet the agriturismo can also perform some ancillary activities for the guests, such as:

- Provide meals
- Provide guides and tours
- Provide entertainment to the guests

In doing so the agriturismo can hire personnel and host clients throughout the whole calendar year (no seasonality requirement); in any case, the agricultural activity must be predominant in respect to the hospitality ones.

How to setup your agriturismo?

In order to setup you agriturismo you must:

- Set up a Partita IVA
- Obtain the *comune* authorization (SCIA)
- Register at the Chamber of Commerce

- Register at the INPS

A successful filing will require you to be a professional farmer with no criminal charges (nor pending charges) whose property passed a hygiene authority inspection.

Once you complete those steps, you can start having guests!

Depending on the Region in which your agriturismo is established, there might be funding available; moreover, you must be aware that often times, the number of rooms and guests are regulated by the regional authorities. This can harm your possibility to scale up your business, as there will be a limit on the number of guests you can serve at one time.

Since agriturismo is considered an agricultural activity, you can take advantage of multiple tax breaks for such activity.

There are two applicable regimes to agriturismo, the ordinary and the *forfettario*. The ordinary regime requires income to be determined on the accrual basis, just like any other type of business, while the *forfettario* regime forfeits the taxable income to 25% of annual turnover.

This means that if you made € 50.000,00 during that year in revenue, you will pay tax only on € 12.500,00 regardless on the amount of costs incurred.

The agriturismo will charge VAT at 10%. If you opt for the ordinary regime you deduct the input VAT from the output VAT, paying any VAT liability.

The *forfettario* forfeits the VAT payable to 50% of the output VAT.

From the previous example, the VAT payable is € 5.000,00, regardless of the actual amount of input VAT deductible.

Moreover, since the *forfettario* regime calls for a simplification of your accounting and tax burden, you have to keep fewer statutory books, reducing then your annual accountant expenditure.

Finally, I would also like to point out that since the agriturismo is an agricultural activity, you can have access to the agricultural financing funds and grants allowing you to have better than market financing conditions.

CASA VACANZE

The "casa vacanze" becomes a mandatory professional activity if you own more than three apartment units in each municipality being leased for hospitality purposes; this regulation of course excludes the long-term rents. In any other case the "casa vacanze" is an option.

Every Region has a different set of rules to regulate the "casa vacanze" and each municipality has the power to control such rulings.

According to the National law the "casa vacanze" is a hospitality structure allowing tourists to stay for periods not exceeding three months; as a "casa vacanze" you cannot offer any other service than hospitality. Furthermore, this activity can be professional as well as occasional.

The property in which you wish to establish your "casa vacanze" needs to be compliant with the most recent energetic, structural, and seismic requirements; usually these requirements are the same as residential properties.

Despite no ruling well defines what an occasional form of business is, there are various tribunal cases defining the occasional activity as such if performed for not the most part of year, with no employees, nor any type of centralized services.

If you do not meet the previously mentioned criteria, or if you manage more than three apartments in one municipality, you are considered a professional.

As a professional you must:

- Set up a Partita IVA
- Obtain the *comune* authorization (SCIA)
- Register at the Chamber of Commerce

- Register at the INPS

You also need to register at the local Questura and keep the registrar of the guests to be sent to the office once a month; this is required for anti-terrorism purposes.

AFFITTACAMERE

The "affittacamere" is another form of hospitality and is defined by the law as a property with no more than 12 beds in 6 rooms. It is possible to provide ancillary services to the hosts.

The only difference between an "affittacamere" and a B&B is the breakfast service, which is absent in the affittacamere.

This activity can be occasional or professional; as an occasional activity you can only let rooms in the same property in which you are registered as a resident, and you have no requirements to meet but to file your annual tax return including such income in the occasional work income.

As a professional you can rent rooms in any property, regardless of your residency. In order to start as a professional affitacamere you must:

- Set up your Partita IVA
- Register at the Chamber of Commerce
- Get the Comune authorization (SCIA)
- Register at INPS

On top of that, you must register at the local Questura and report any guest within 48 hours of their arrival.

The best part about the "affittacamere" is that you can opt for the "regime forfettario" that does not charge any VAT and provides a reduced tax rate of 5% for the first 5 years of business, as long as you make less than € 50.000,00 per year.

Assuming you make such income, your taxable income will be just 40% of the total revenue (regardless of the expenses you incurred), hence € 20.000,00. Therefore, your tax liability is just € 1.000,00 for the next 5 years.

Total Revenue	€ 50.000,00
Taxable Income	€ 20.000,00
Tax rate	5 %
Tax paid	**€ 1.000,00**

B&B

The Italian law defines B&B as a hospitality provided in private premises including breakfast. The number of guests cannot exceed 20 units and, depending on the Regional rules, the maximum number of rooms varies from three to six.

According to our tax authorities, B&B is not a commercial nor professional activity, thus you do not need to setup your Partita IVA nor pay Social Security to the INPS and register at the local Chamber of Commerce. As a non-commercial activity, the law requires each B&B not to operate for at least three months per year.

In order to setup your B&B, you need first to have residency in the B&B premises, then you need to file a SCIA (authorization request) to your local municipality, requesting the opening of the B&B; on top of that, you need to communicate to the local Questura the guests ID that stayed at your place.

Once you have cleared the above checkpoints, you can operate as a B&B, receiving guests.

You are required to issue a receipt to the guests.

In your tax return you must include all the receipts issued and the deductible expenses receipt, doing that allows you to pay taxes on your profit.

In this chapter, I have shown you multiple options to make the most out of your property. The best way to achieve all these steps is to be assisted step by step by your tax accountant that can help you out in ascertaining the best business form, setting up your business, and maintaining the annual tax compliance.

Esterovestizione

Esterovestizione is very difficult to translate. Referring to a foreign company or entity, this means that your company is wrongfully incorporated abroad according to the Italian tax laws.

We all know that Italy is a high tax jurisdiction, and many individuals do not feel comfortable to pay taxes to the Italian government and usually they come up with a simple solution: let all your income be made through a foreign incorporated Limited company. Economy giants such as Google, Facebook, and others do that, why shouldn't you?

You can find plenty of services securing discretion and privacy on the Internet that will help you incorporate your business wherever you want! In a couple of clicks you can now be the shareholder of your own offshore shell company. It is an easy and painless process.

From now on, you should not worry about Italian taxes anymore. Not so fast...

The Italian tax law is very clear about this topic as it considers Italian resident any company that has any of the following in Italy:

- Registered address;
- Administrative address
- Main activity.

While you will never be so naïve to incorporate a company abroad and register its address in Italy, you must be aware that if you either have your main clients in Italy or an administrative address here, the company falls under the *esterovestizione*.

According to the Italian law if the majority part of the administrative organisation is resident in Italy, the company has its administrative address there, unless you can prove that managing decision where taken elsewhere. Good luck!

What are the penalties?

The penalties are extremely harsh if you do not pay any income tax, VAT, Social Security, on top of the penalties for every missing tax return.

You are required to pay every penny of unpaid tax on top of fines ranging from 120% up to 240% of unpaid taxes, and if you end up owing more than € 30.000,00 you will face criminal charges.

At this point, the most common question is: how can they find me?

First of all, the Chamber of Commerce registrars are public, and in some jurisdictions (like the UK) are online and free.

Furthermore, OECD countries signed exchange information treaties in which they exchange taxpayers' information, especially information related to shell corporations.

Finally, if you invoice any Italian client, it is required to report such transaction to the Italian tax authorities making you available in the tax office systems.

Once they catch you, the tax authorities can go back up to 8 years and request all unpaid taxes.

Unfortunately, I have assisted many clients once they were caught by the tax authorities in one of the three aforementioned ways, and all I could do is work to minimize the fines applied.

It should be known that it is possible to keep your business in a country other than Italy, all you have to know is that this move requires care to be taken in order to avoid any unpleasant surprise in the future, and to ensure that the setup and operations of any legal entities tied to you name explicitly follow the law.

As a tax accountant, I have been assisting multiple business owners in their transition to the Italian jurisdiction, and I have to say that with the proper actions, risks can be reduced to zero.

My advice to you is to discuss your tax situation with an experienced tax accountant in this field.

Rent-to-buy guide

Rent-to-Buy is a recent formula to purchase property in Italy. Introduced in 2009, rent to buy has seen moderate success in Italy. Below are the main features of Rent-to-Buy.

The Rent-to-Buy logic is very simple; the prospect buyer lives in the house he will purchase later, and the lease agreement eventually turns into a property sale. Rent-to-Buy is not a form of financing.

The contract allows the buyer to use the property now and to purchase it in the future at a price defined today. There is no possibility to negotiate a different price in the future. Up to the property transfer, the seller remains the owner of the property.

I like to define the Rent-to-Buy as a gradual payment.

The rent to buy contract revolves around two main periods:

- Renting period
- Buying period

The renting period can last up to 10 years; in this period the buyer can use the property while paying rent. The rent is then split into two different parts: the actual rent and the advance payment.

The law does not require a minimum or maximum amount of monthly (or quarterly) payment and the fraction counts towards the house advance payment.

The agreement states the deed date, but it is possible that the parties can agree on an earlier date. The designated buyer is the one who signs the agreement, thus the seller cannot sell the property to a third individual.

A penalty is usually enforced if any party withdrawals from the agreement prior to the transaction. Regarding the property, there are several main reasons to adopt the Rent-to-Buy scheme:

1. Allow the buyer to gather enough financial resources to apply for a loan.

2. Allow the buyer to sell realize the sale of a third property before buying the new one.
3. If you wish to buy property with a company you usually need a history of three years to apply for a loan. In such case you can sign the rent to buy and apply for a loan later down the road.
4. Buy a new activity (hotel, restaurant, agriturismo, B&B) and sustain the payments with the operating cash flow.

Rent-to-buy can be a fantastic option providing flexibility to both parties, and it gathered great success with all types of property; land, residential, commercial, non-residential etc.

In Italy you can sign two types of Rent-to-Buy agreements.

ORIGINAL RENT-TO-BUY

This contract form dates back to 2009. This Rent-to-Buy consist in two different contracts:

1. Preliminary property sale contract
2. Lease contract

Both contracts are registered at the *Agenzia delle Entrate* in order to avoid any potential anti-abuse ruling as well as the *Catasto*, protecting the buyer from the following scenario:

- Seller's bankruptcy
- Seller's death
- Third party foreclosure

In this scenario the buyer and the seller agree on the future price of the property and the deed date signing the preliminary contract.

Usually, the seller asks for a lump sum to be paid at signature of the contract.

Both parties then sign a lease contract. The lease payment is divided in two parts, one part goes toward the payment for the property, while the other is the rent per se.

At deed date, the buyer will pay the seller the agreed price, deducting the lump sum and the monthly contributions already paid.

RECENT RENT TO BUY

This contract was introduced in 2014, and it is a single contract instead of two like the original rent to buy.

In such scenario, both parties agree on a deed date and on a set price for the property. On top of that, the parties agree on the monthly payments and its subdivision between rent and property contribution.

This new Rent-to-Buy does not allow for a lump sum to be paid in advance and allows greater flexibility as the property can be purchased up to the deed date.

Rent-to-Buy is a great opportunity to get involved in the real estate market. Unfortunately, many sellers do not want to use Rent-to-But due to a lack of understanding of such a tool.

APPENDIX

IRPEF

Imposta sul Reddito delle Persone Fisiche, the Italian income tax

IRPEF BRACKETS

INCOME	TAX RATE
Up to € 15.000	23%
From € 15.001 to € 28.000	27%
From € 28.001 to € 55.000	38%
From € 55.001 to € 75.000	41%
Above € 75.001	43%

IRES

Imposta sul Reddito delle Societa, Corporation tax

IRAP

Imposta Regionale Attività Produttive, Regional corporation tax surcharge

PARTITA IVA

VAT number in Italy

CODICE FISCALE

Personal tax number in Italy

SCIA

Segnalazione Certificata Inizio Attività, municipality authorization to start any activity

CAMERA DI COMMERCIO

Chamber of Commerce

GEOMETRA

Italian professional expert in constructions and cadastre

NOTAIO

Italian public notary is the official that signs and authorizes the property deeds

AGENZIA DELLE ENTRATE

Italian tax and revenue service

COMUNE

Town hall

Printed in Great Britain
by Amazon